T0419291

PANAMA CANAL

BY BRIENNA ROSSITER

Apex is distributed by North Star Editions:
sales@northstareditions.com | 888-417-0195

Produced for Apex by Red Line Editorial.

Photographs ©: Shutterstock Images, cover, 1, 4–5, 6, 7, 8–9, 10–11, 12, 13, 14–15, 18, 19, 20, 21, 22–23, 26–27, 27, 29; Library of Congress, 16–17; Warren K. Leffler/Library of Congress, 24

Library of Congress Control Number: 2023910873

ISBN
978-1-63738-751-1 (hardcover)
978-1-63738-794-8 (paperback)
978-1-63738-878-5 (ebook pdf)
978-1-63738-837-2 (hosted ebook)

Printed in the United States of America
Mankato, MN
012024

NOTE TO PARENTS AND EDUCATORS

Apex books are designed to build literacy skills in striving readers. Exciting, high-interest content attracts and holds readers' attention. The text is carefully leveled to allow students to achieve success quickly. Additional features, such as bolded glossary words for difficult terms, help build comprehension.

TABLE OF CONTENTS

CHAPTER 1

A BIG SHORTCUT

A ship floats through the Panama **Canal**. It is coming from the Atlantic Ocean. The ship enters a set of **locks**.

Ships use the Panama Canal to travel between the Atlantic Ocean and Pacific Ocean.

More than 26 million gallons (98 million L) of water floods into the locks to raise ships.

The locks fill with water. That causes the ship to slowly rise. Eventually, the water level reaches 85 feet (26 m) above sea level. Then the ship moves through Gatún Lake.

FAST FACT

Gatún Lake makes up about half of the canal.

Gatún Lake is 20 miles (32 km) long.

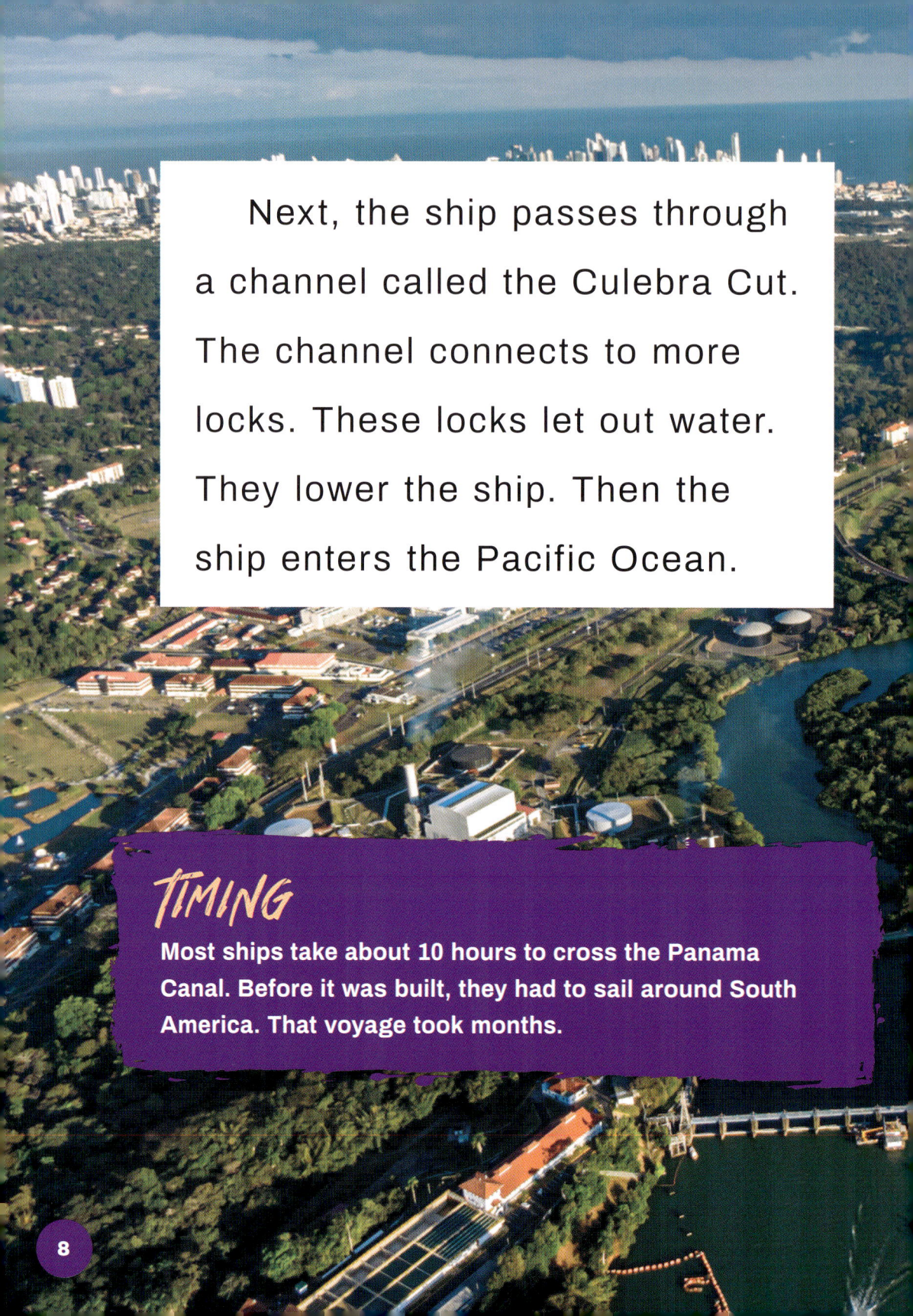

Next, the ship passes through a channel called the Culebra Cut. The channel connects to more locks. These locks let out water. They lower the ship. Then the ship enters the Pacific Ocean.

TIMING

Most ships take about 10 hours to cross the Panama Canal. Before it was built, they had to sail around South America. That voyage took months.

After the Culebra Cut, two sets of locks lower ships to sea level.

CHAPTER 2

HOW IT WORKS

Panama is an **isthmus** in Central America. The canal cuts across the country. It uses locks to bring ships over a mountain range.

Panama is the narrowest part of Central America. It separates the Atlantic and the Pacific Oceans.

The locks are each 1,000 feet (305 m) long and 110 feet (34 m) wide.

Each lock has two huge gates. One gate lets ships in. Then the water level changes to match the canal's next section. Ships leave the lock through the second gate.

LARGE LAKE

Some of the locks get water from Gatún Lake. People made this lake by building a dam on the Chagres River. The dam caused a huge area of land to flood.

The dam that created Gatún Lake is 115 feet (35 m) high. It is called Gatún Dam.

Train engines run along the walls of each lock. They guide big ships. They keep the ships from hitting gates or walls.

The train engines are attached to ships with chains.

FAST FACT

The locks are built in pairs. That way, ships can go opposite ways at the same time.

CHAPTER 3

BUILDING THE CANAL

n the 1800s, several countries wanted to dig a canal across Central America. A French company tried. But it ran out of money and failed.

By the late 1800s, steam-powered ships carried many products across the ocean.

Workers used 102 steam shovels to construct the Panama Canal.

The US government bought this company. It took over the project. Building began in 1904. Workers used steam shovels and **dynamite**. They carved through hills and mountains.

Railroads transported dirt used to build the Gatún Dam.

Panama has many mosquitoes. These insects can spread deadly diseases.

Panama's rainy weather made the work challenging. It caused **landslides** and made workers sick. Even so, the canal was finished by 1914.

CULEBRA CUT

Culebra Cut was the hardest part to make. Workers blasted through 9 miles (14 km) of mountains. Several times, landslides filled the cut in. Digging had to start over.

About 40,000 people worked on the Panama Canal. At least 5,000 died.

CHAPTER 4

THROUGH THE YEARS

At first, the United States owned the Panama Canal. It also controlled an area around it. This was because of a **treaty** with Panama.

Many ships began to use the Panama Canal. The US-controlled area was known as the Canal Zone.

Over time, Panama gained more control. After 1999, it owned the canal and the land around it.

A NEW COUNTRY

In 1903, Panama was part of Colombia. US leaders tried making a deal with Colombia. When that didn't work, they helped Panama become **independent**. Then they worked with Panama.

In 1977, President Jimmy Carter (right) signed treaties to give Panama control of the canal.

The canal became a key part of trade. Thousands of ships use it each year. They come from many countries. And they carry tons of **cargo**.

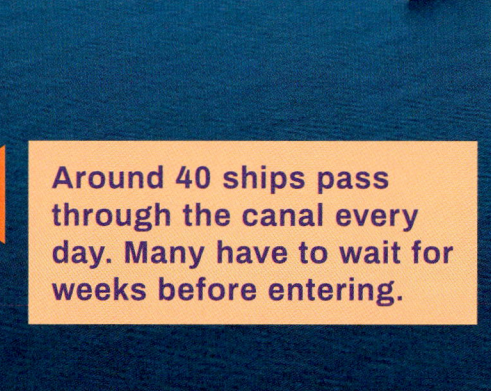

Around 40 ships pass through the canal every day. Many have to wait for weeks before entering.

Ships pay a toll to go through the canal. This money goes to Panama.

COMPREHENSION
QUESTIONS

Write your answers on a separate piece of paper.

1. Write a few sentences describing how ships move through the Panama Canal.

2. What fact about the Panama Canal did you find most impressive? Why?

3. When did the United States begin building the canal?

    A. 1904

    B. 1914

    C. 1999

4. What would happen if the canal had single locks instead of pairs?

    A. Ships could no longer travel through.

    B. Ships could only go one way at a time.

    C. The way ships use the canal would not change.

5. What does **voyage** mean in this book?

*Before it was built, they had to sail around South America. That **voyage** took months.*

    A. a way to get somewhere
    B. a way to make money
    C. a try to trick someone

6. What does **challenging** mean in this book?

*Panama's rainy weather made the work **challenging**. It caused landslides and made workers sick.*

    A. easy to do
    B. full of problems
    C. free from problems

Answer key on page 32.

GLOSSARY

canal
A narrow, human-made waterway that connects to other bodies of water.

cargo
Items carried by a plane, ship, train, or truck from one place to another.

dynamite
A type of strong explosive used to blast through rock.

independent
Not ruled or controlled by another country.

isthmus
A thin strip of land that connects two large areas of land.

landslides
Times when rocks and dirt slide quickly down a hill or mountain, burying things in their path.

locks
Parts of a waterway that raise or lower boats between levels.

treaty
An agreement between two or more countries or groups.

TO LEARN MORE

BOOKS

Goldish, Meish. *Panama*. New York: Bearport Publishing, 2020.

Klepeis, Alicia Z. *Panama*. Minneapolis: Bellwether Media, 2023.

McAneney, Caitie. *20 Fun Facts About Famous Canals and Seaways*. New York: Gareth Stevens Publishing, 2020.

ONLINE RESOURCES

Visit **www.apexeditions.com** to find links and resources related to this title.

ABOUT THE AUTHOR

Brienna Rossiter is a writer and editor who lives in Minnesota.

INDEX

ANSWER KEY:
1. Answers will vary; 2. Answers will vary; 3. A; 4. B; 5. A; 6. B